THE PARODY PROJECT

Created by,

Ronald A. Busse

Second Edition
Printed in the United States of America

ISBN 978-1-969818-27-1 (Hardcover)
ISBN 978-1-969818-26-4 (Paperback)
ISBN 978-1-969818-25-7 (Digital)

CREDITS

Afif Aulia: interior illustrations and cover art. Interested in hiring Afif? Contact him on Instagram @apivv, or by email @suwwarna@gmail.com.

Crystal Whittenburg: author photograph

SOURCES

While most of the musical facts and statistics in the notes following each parody were obtained from *Billboard*, some were obtained from other online sources. Most of these and all *Billboard* facts and stats were retrieved from Wikipedia.

My primary source for finding songs to parody was *Rolling Stone* magazine's list of "The 500 Greatest Songs of All Time." Song lyrics were obtained from www.AZLyrics.com. And many Google searches were conducted.

ACKNOWLEDGMENTS

I would like to thank "Weird Al" Yankovic, whose influence and inspiration were a constant presence as I wrote the song lyric parodies you are about to read.

Special thanks to my brother, Jeff Busse, for his creative input, help, and ideas; to my special friends, sisters Nancy Neira and Sandy Keller, for their song suggestions and for being my best audience; and also to Nancy for her terrific idea for "Pizza Burnin'"; and to my niece, Nicole Busse, for her ingenious Photoshop skills!

I would also like to thank the following publications for introducing some of my song lyric parodies to the world in advance of this release:

For the Many Not the Few anthology, based in Scotland, and its editor, CT Meek, for publishing "Feet Ache," "Fairfield's Burning," and "Rollin' Down the Gutter" in Volume 43, Spring 2025.

Tigershark Magazine, based in England, and its editor, DS Davidson, for publishing "Our Crypt's Unsealed" in Issue Thirty-Four, Autumn/Winter 2023, Alternative Times theme.

CRM Enterprises e-Newsletter and its editor, Celine Rose Mariotti, for publishing "Haunted Haystack" and "Our Crypt's Unsealed" in the September/October 2023 edition, and "Let's Get a Physical" in the October 2022 edition.

I also wish to recognize *Drunken Pen Writing* for accepting "Haunted Haystack" in September 2022, prior to their unexpected shutdown before it could be published.

This project is lovingly dedicated

in memory of my dad,

Ronald W. Busse

September 11, 1941 to May 15, 2024

TABLE OF CONTENTS

PARODY OVERVIEW

DEFINITION

Parody

[**par**-*uh*-dee]

As a **noun**, a parody is a comical or satirical imitation of a serious piece of literature, poetry, or form of entertainment.

As a **verb**, to parody means to imitate, mock, or poke fun at a written or musical composition, author, TV show, et cetera, for purposes of laughter, irony, satire, or even ridicule.

ORIGIN

It is said that in ancient Greece, a parody was a song or poem that imitated the style and flow of another song or poem. The word parody is comprised of the Greek root words *par*, meaning "beside," and *ody*, referring to an "ode" or "song."

A NOD TO "WEIRD AL"

Today, music continues to be a popular form of parody. Probably the best-known song parody artist is **"Weird Al" Yankovic**, who makes his living by creating parodies of popular music. Among his most famous song parodies are "Eat It," "Amish Paradise," "Gump," "Another One Rides the Bus," "Tacky," "Like a Surgeon," and his first single, "My Bologna," released in 1979.

FORWARD

Welcome to my chapbook of song lyric parodies!

It is filled with funny and, at times, nonsensical alternate lyrics to popular songs, interwoven with elements of poetry; created to induce smiles and laughter, and bring a bit of senseless joy to a complicated, chaotic world.

Each parody is built around a specific topic. Food is a recurring theme, from pizza to nachos to hollandaise sauce, and the legendary sitcom *Seinfeld* is a catalyst for a few unique parodies. Other topics include being hopelessly lost at sea, a "routine" doctor's appointment, some dude who wishes food were beer, Halloween, a woman whose shoes don't (and won't) fit, a dog that thinks it's a farm animal, and a boxer who can't (or won't) stay on his feet.

As I wrote my first couple of parodies, I discovered that by singing the music in my head as I read along with the parodied lyrics, the words and lines flowed better with the imaginary music. I encourage you to try this, as doing so is likely to enhance your reading experience, which I hope will be fun and amusing!

An Odd Dog's Life

A parody of the song "A Hard Day's Night" *by the Beatles*

It's been an odd dog's life
Had my upbringing on a farm
I lead an odd dog's life
It has me squealing like a hog
And when I woof, I go moo
At dawn, cock-a-doodle-doo!
For me, it feels so right

I go berserk all day
Mimicking horses and honeybees
I can't make honey, but it's okay
'Cause I can buzzzz and I can neigh
So watch me drink from a trough
Wallow with pigs in mud, yawp
Oink-oink, curl up my tail, let's play

Throw a bone
I'll sit and watch it take flight
I'll just groan
Fetching no longer excites
Me, nah

It's been an odd dog's life
Grazing in pastures like the cows
I lead an odd dog's life
Baaing with sheep, hooting with owls
On grass and hay, I do chew
Sometimes I sleep in a coop
Cluck with the chickens, pure delight!
(Don't make me lay eggs or I'll bite.)
This farming life's alright!

A gem from the deep well of number-one singles the Beatles amassed in their almost ten years together, "A Hard Day's Night" was also the title of the band's first feature movie. It was released at the height of Beatlemania, on August 11, 1964.

Rollin' Down the Gutter

A parody of the song "Proud Mary" *by Creedence Clearwater Revival*

Left my day job, took up bowling
Workin' on my game ev'ry night and day
But there only was one itsy-bitsy problem,
I can't hit no more than three pins per frame!

My hook, I can't control it
Never know where it's goin'
Rollin',
rollin',
rollin' down the gutter

Jumped a lot of balls into Lane 6
Watched 'em hyperplane down the oily lanes
Missin' spares galore and leavin' lotsa big splits
Split my ball in half, made the 7-10 (legit?)

My ball keeps on swervin'
I know just where it's goin'
Rollin',
rollin',
rollin' in the gutter

Years ago, on *Bowling for Dollars*
My ball went down the lane and so did I!
Knocked down all the pins, but won me no money
People on the set were unhappy as s**t

Only strikes I'm gettin'
Are when the ball hits my knee while swingin'
Rollin',
rollin',
rollin' down the gutter

Rollin',
rollin',
bowlin' lots of gutters
Rollin',
rollin',
hey, I bowled anot'er!

Rollin',
bowlin',
tripped the foul line buzzer!

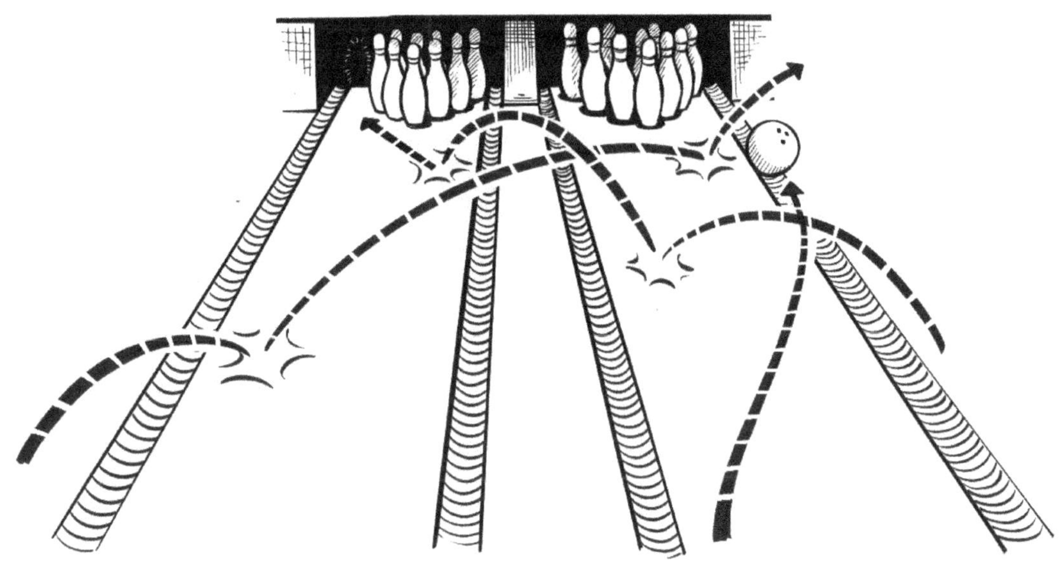

CCR scored their first of five number-two singles with the release of "Proud Mary" in 1969, from their second album, *Bayou Country*. In total, the band hit the *Billboard* Top 10 nine times without ever topping the Hot 100 chart.

Pizza Burnin'

A parody of the song "Beast of Burden" *by the Rolling Stones*

I'll never leave your pizza burnin'
I'll cook it right, my crust is golden
Set my oven—to seven, eight hundred degrees

I'll never leave your pizza burnin'
I've worked all night, so you won't return it
All I want is satisfaction guaranteed

Is it hot enough?
Topped with lots of stuff?
Does it rank above
Domino's delivery?

I'll be your pizza maker servin'
The best you've had; won't leave you burpin'
Sausage, ham, and pineapple
Sure, I'll hold the anchovies

Can I stuff your crust?
Cheese just ain't enough
I will make it bust
With lots of pepperoni!

I'll never leave your pizza burnin',
Nor undercooked. Baked to perfection!
Deep Dish, Grandma, Sicilian, or Baked Ziti

I don't need no recipe learnin'
Make pies from scratch; folks do prefer it
You name it! I'll make it! Pizza for everybody!

Released as the second single from the Rolling Stones' 1978 *Some Girls* album, "Beast of Burden" (a Top 10 *Billboard* Hot 100 hit) was featured in the 1983 movie *Christine*, based on author Stephen King's #1 bestselling novel.

Lost Car

A Seinfeld *parody of the song* "Fast Car" *by Tracy Chapman*

We've got a lost car
Got no plan to get us out of here
Lost in a mall parking garage
The car is somewhere; finding it could take years
There are four colored levels
But we forgot which is ours
Everything looks the same!
We're like rats in some experiment, George did say—

We've got a lost car
Me and George, we really had to pee
With nowhere else to go,
Peed in a dark corner, got arrested, but me
I tried to explain I could get
Uromysitisis poisoning and die
But the cop wasn't buying
So we paid the ticket, went back to the garage—

We've got a lost car
Looking for hours while Elaine's fish die
They can't live in a plastic bag
More than a couple hours and it's goodbye
Kramer bought a big A/C
(It's the actual thing, not an empty box.)
Almost dropped it when he hid it
Behind another car in Purple 23—

And so the search went on and on, wandering around
Aimlessly, no car to be found
Was it Orange 4C or Blue 15?
Is the car anywhere or did it disappear?
And ai-yai-yai! When we asked some folks, can you drive us around?
They-y-y said things like sorry, can't do it or laughed, ignoring us—

We've got a lost car
George's parents waiting on their anniversary
Won't get there by 6:15
Now dinner won't be eaten; the show unseen
And he knows it's gonna kill them

On the biggest night of their lives
Furious as they will be,
They'll put George on an aggravation installment plan...

And so the search went on and on, was it Yellow 3?
Green 22, Blue 24D?
Three of us couldn't remember,
Elaine wasn't paying any attention
And ai-yai-yai! When we finally found the car
I-*i*-*i* had a feeling we'd get out of here, out of here, out of here...?

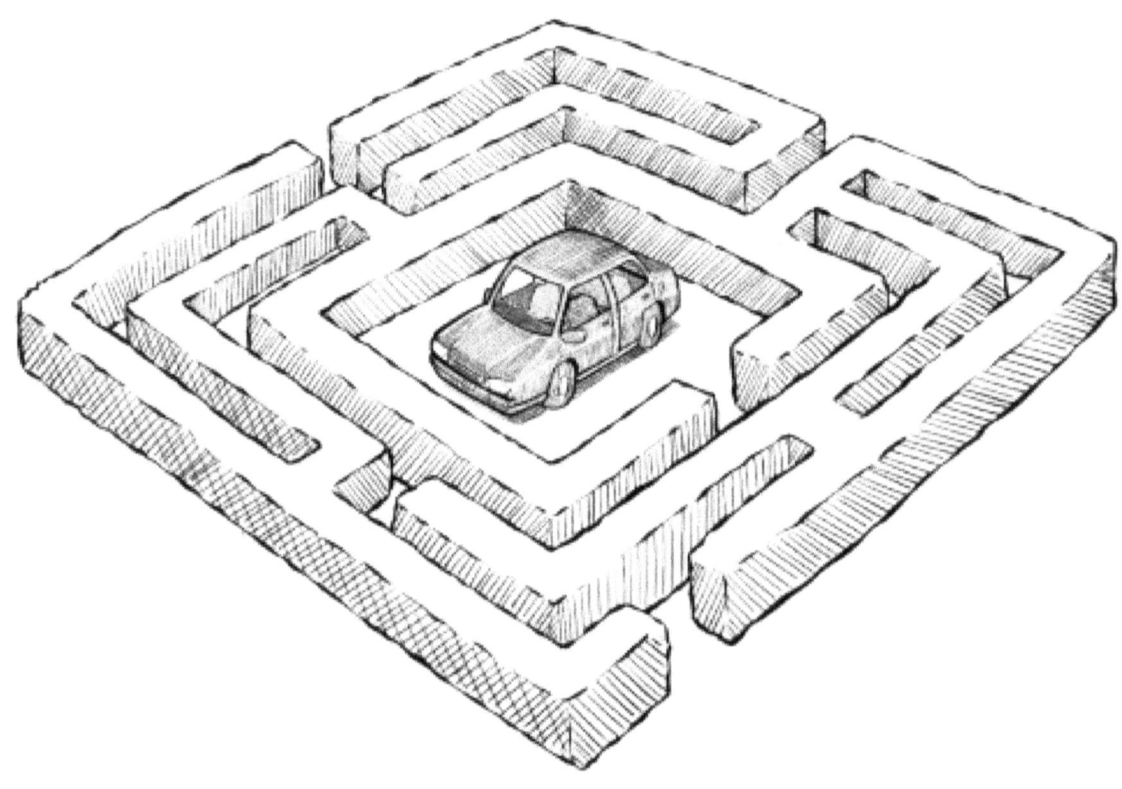

Told from Jerry Seinfeld's point of view, this is a parody of the hilarious *Seinfeld*, Season 3 episode "The Parking Garage." In this episode, all four main characters – Jerry, George, Elaine, and Kramer—are stuck in the same predicament: they can't find the car. At the end, when they finally do find the car, it won't start. This mishap was not written in the script. "The Parking Garage" was the first *Seinfeld* episode recorded without a live audience.

I Want to Know Romance

A parody of the song "I Want to Hold Your Hand" *by the Beatles*

So sad, I got that nothing
You may not understand
When I say sweet nothings
You won't give me a chance

I wanna know ro-ma-a-a-ance
I wanna know romance

Say please, I'm not a sleaze
Swear I'm a reformed man
Let me serenade thee
I'll be your one-man band

Reach out and take my ha-a-a-and
Now may I have this dance?

Of when you'll touch me, I think happy
Thoughts inside
It's just my dream of feeling love
That I hide
Deep inside
Where I *cryyyy*

Yeah, I got that nothing
That makes you turn your glance
Then I say that wrong thing
Won't you forget my past?

I'll show you charm and cla-a-a-as
Wine and dine you in France

I wanna know ro-ma-a-a-a-a-ance

Kicking off the British Invasion in early 1964, "I Want to Hold Your Hand" was the Fab Four's first American number-one single on the Billboard Hot 100 chart, where it spent seven weeks – only to be dethroned by its follow-up, "She Loves You."

Nacho Stand

A parody of the song "Macho Man" *by the Village People*

Hungry
Gotta fill my tummy
Grandé
Nachos thrill my tummy's
Rumbly
Hunger pangs, crave something
Yummy
Nachos in my tummy

Every stand ought to be an all-night nacho stand
That serves the kind of Nachos Supreme I so demand
Drivin' 'cross the country, go man go
Passin' lemonade stands, no man, no
You can best believe I need a nacho stand
On every single corner, in every single land
Maine! Spain! Zim-bab-we!

Nacho, nacho stand
I gotta find a nacho stand
Fried, baked, fresh, or canned
I gotta get some nachos!

You can smell the nachos, globs of gooey cheese
Topped with jalapeños and blobs of sour cream
Take your choice of proteins, pork or beef
Or chicken, you know what? I'll take all three
You can best believe I need a nacho stand
And if I cannot find one, I'll build my own instead
¡Vi-sí-ta-nos hoy!

Nacho, nacho stand
I gotta find my Nacholand
Stop at every stand
I gotta eat more nachos!

Released in 1978, "Macho Man" was the first charting hit single for the costumed Village People. It was first parodied by feathered singer Donald Duck, who recorded "Macho Duck" for the Disney album *Mickey Mouse Disco* in 1979. I did my best to follow in his webbed footsteps.

Rockin' Around the Aluminum Pole

A Seinfeld *parody of the song* "Rockin' Around the Christmas Tree" *by Brenda Lee*

Rockin' around the aluminum pole
Have a Happy Festivus!
Frank and George compete in the Feats of Strength
On this day for the rest of us

Rockin' around the aluminum pole
No tinsel to distract
Gwen shows up, but the lighting's bad
A Festivus miracle gone splat

You will air your grievances
'Cause Frank's got problems with you
We know things are getting bad
When Kruger pulls out his whiskey flask

Rockin' around the aluminum pole
Have a Happy Festivus!
'Out there' or not this holiday
Is for the rest of us!

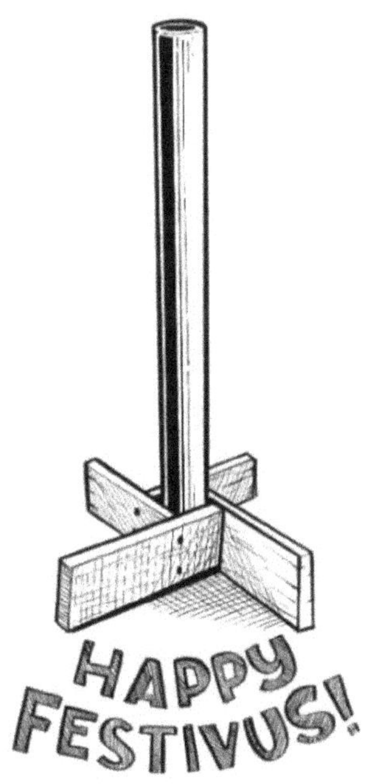

These alternate lyrics are based on the historic *Seinfeld*, Season 9 episode, "The Strike," in which Frank Costanza's made-up holiday, Festivus, was made famous. This is the first parody I wrote.

Simpson, Jay Homer

A parody of The Simpsons, *of the song* "Crimson and Clover"
by Tommy James and the Shondells

D'oh!
They say my first name is Homer
And I ain't never sober
Duff beer and donuts (Mmmm, donuts...)

Hiccup!
And when I go waddling to Moe's
I listen to Grand Funk Railroad
Duff beer and donuts
Over and over

'urrrp!
My Marge is like Margarine
And I hate stupid Flanders
What a cringe-able feeling
Patty and Selma
Smoking over and over

Duff beer and donuts
Over and over

Duff beer and donuts
I'm "Dancin' Homer"

Duff beer and donuts
Prank monkey Homer

Duff beer and donuts
"Hungry, Hungry Homer"

Duff beer and donuts
I'm "King-Size Homer"

Duff beer and donuts
Drink a Flaming Homer

Duff beer and donuts
Me "Deep Space Homer"

Duff beer and donuts
Under and– *D'oh!*

Homer Simpson lets loose in this parody of *The Simpsons*, the longest-running animated sitcom TV series in America. Now in its 37th season and 801st episode (as of December 14, 2025), *The Simpsons* first appeared in a series of animated short films that aired as a recurring segment on *The Tracey Ullman Show* beginning in 1987. The show's first episode, the Christmas-themed *Simpsons Roasting on an Open Fire*, debuted on December 17, 1989.

The "Hole In One (or Two)"

A The Price Is Right *parody of the song* "Theme from The Brady Bunch" *by The Brady Bunch*

Feel the glory
Of winning "Squeeze Play,"
Cars on "Cover Up,"
Three strings of lovely pearls
Going down the "Golden Road,"
"Any Number,"
Give the Big Wheel a whirl!

Hit the "Bullseye"
"10 Chances," "Grand Game"
"To The Penny"
Get "3 Strikes" and hear trombones
Guess "Now Or Then"
Winning "Pick-A-Number"
"Let 'Em Roll" and "Plinko"

Tilt the "Balance Game,"
"Triple Play," "More Or Less," "Hi Lo"
Double overbid's
The worst, let's "Pass The Buck,"
"Switcheroo"
Come On Down!, we're a family
"One Away," the "Money Game"
and "Punch A Bunch"

Yell "That's Too Much!"
It's fun to watch
Drew Carey and George Gray –
Win a "Vend-O-Price" lunch!

The wildly popular game show *The Price Is Right* originally aired in 1956 and was hosted by Bill Cullen until 1965. The show was revived in 1972 and was hosted by the charming Bob Barker, until his retirement in 2007. Since then, comedian and actor Drew Carey has been carrying the microphone on the longest-running game show in the United States. Winner of 49 Daytime Emmy Awards, *The Price Is Right* aired its 10,000th episode on February 26, 2025. This parody names 25 of the many fun pricing games played on the show.

OUR CRYPT'S UNSEALED

A parody of the song "Our Lips Are Sealed" *by the Go-Go's*

Can you hear us?
We haunt about you
Groaning sighs
Invisible disguise

You can't see us
You see through us
Though we weigh nil
Don't doubt that we are real

You can't chase us, we won't go away
Twisted Sister, we came out to play
Blue skies gray!
Our crypt's unsealed

The lid's open
We're on the loose
Hear our lament
Dirges of boos

When we spook you
Fear flies through you
See how we disappear
Only to reappear

Scare your pants off, let them run away
We don't want them anyway
You're our prey!
Our crypt's unsealed

Whooshing...looping
We terrify
Swooping...swooshing
We terrorize

Slam the lid, nail it down and pray
The crypt creeps open anyway
Run away!
Our crypt's unsealed
Evil's revealed
When our crypt's unsealed!

The Go-Go's burst onto the L.A. punk rock scene in the late 70s before releasing their first album, *Beauty and the Beat*, in 1981, which contained their first single, "Our Lips Are Sealed." The album spent six weeks atop the *Billboard* album chart, making it the first number-one album by an all-female band writing their own songs and playing their own instruments.

Takin' a Dive

A parody of the song "Stayin' Alive" *by the Bee Gees*

Well, you can tell by the way I punch and block
I'm a wuss, I am; no guts, I fall
"1!"

Bruises, blood, stars spin in swarms
I get knocked around, not so adorned
"2!"

And now it's not alright, not okay
You'll want to look the other way
I don't try; have to pretend
My jabs can hurt a weaker man
"3!"

Never been a winner
I'm every time a loser
I'm takin' a dive, takin' a dive
Feel my body achin'
And every bone breakin'
I'll be stayin' alive by takin' a dive

Aye, yai, yai, I'm takin' a dive, takin' a dive
Aye, yai, yai, I'm takin' a d*iii*-
iii-
iiii-
iiii-
*i*ve...
Goin' down!
"4!"

I deke low, I cut high
And when I miss my mark, I get a black eye
"5!"

Got the sting of leather, black-and-blue
I'm a divin' man, I can't help but lose
"6!"

And now it's alright, it's okay
I'll live to fight another day

'Cause I go down, it's all been planned
My fans throw half-filled beer cans
"7!"

Never been a winner
I'm every time a loser
I'm takin' a dive, takin' a dive
Feel my body achin'
And every bone breakin'
I'll be stayin' alive by takin' a dive
"8!"

Aye, yai, yai, I'm takin' a dive, takin' a dive
Aye, yai, yai, I'm takin' a d*iii*-
iii-
iiii-
iiii-
*i*ve...
"9!"
Life spinnin', blank stare. Nobody help me
Just let me fall, yeah
Prizewinning ne'er. Head hits the canvas
I'm takin' a d*iiiiii*ve
"10!
YOU'RE OUT!"

From the *Saturday Night Fever* soundtrack, "Stayin' Alive" was the second of six consecutive number-one *Billboard* hit singles, from 1977 to 1979, for the unstoppable Brothers Gibb. The other five were "How Deep Is Your Love" and "Night Fever," also from *Saturday Night Fever*, followed by "Tragedy," "Too Much Heaven," and "Love You Inside Out" from the *Spirits Having Flown* album.

Let's Get a Physical

A parody of the song "Physical" *by Olivia Newton-John*

You're saying fancy terms, making it sound like
I need a major operation
I gotta handle on my life
Your talk sounds Greek to me

Your blood pressure machine squeezes my arm too hard
Then you take a hammer to my knee
What's all the fuss, am I going mad?
I'm okay mentally

Let's get a physical, physical
You know it's only practical
To go and get a physical
Listen to your body-talk, your body-talk
Listen to your doctor talk

I've been your patient since childhood
We know each other intimately
I stick my tongue out, "ahhh," and gag
And you want me quarantined!

I'm sure results will show that I don't have the flu
Bubonic plague, mumps, or diabetes
You gotta know that although I'm fine
I'll see you bimonthly

Let's get a physical, physical
You know it's only logical
To go and get a physical
Listen to your body-talk, your body-talk
Let your doctor poke and prod

Get your annual, annual
Rely not on a manual
It's been a year, no doubt, now, call
Listen to your body-talk
Wind your biological clock...

"Physical" was first offered to Tina Turner, then Rod Stewart. When they both turned it down, Olivia Newton-John took it to number one on the *Billboard* Hot 100 chart, where it stayed for a then-record-tying 10 weeks. It went on to become the number one song of 1982.

Wish Food Were Beer

A parody of the song "Wish You Were Here" *by Pink Floyd*

No-o-o, you wouldn't be able to tell
Melons from Modelo
Blue Moon from romaine
Couldn't tell a green bean field
From a cold Steel Reserve
French fries from an ale
Do you think it would sell?

Just think if they could ma-a-a-ake
Boarshead heroes as Michelob
Hot knishes as brewskis
Hot fare as hops and yeast,
cold water and grains
All food would be cha-a-anged
A chocolate croissant becomes Coors
Pour a mug, stein, pitcher, or keg

How I wish,
How I wish food were beer
We would drink our Cheerios from a big beer bowl,
Beer after beer
Hiccuping as we stumble around
"We'll have a rou-ou-ou-ound
of pickle spears!"
Wish food were beer...

"Wish You Were Here," the dark title track from Pink Floyd's 1975 concept album, was the English rock band's ninth studio release. Its lyrics, in part, are a tribute to founder and former bandmate, Syd Barrett.

Vincent's Picks

A Seinfeld *parody of the song* "Vincent" *by Don McLean*

Movie rental night
Flicks from Champagne Video
Colin, Gene, Elizabeth
And other staffers' picks hang on the wall

None compare at all
To Vincent's picks, they're all so great
How *The Pain and the Yearning* relates
To pain and yearning for three hours straight

They don't understand
What your movies mean to me
And how you suffer from your acne
You cannot bear to be seen

All that yearning made me cry and bellow,
"Bravo, Vincent! Bra-*vo!*"

Movie rental night
A Vincent's pick all set to play
The Other Woman, I can't wait
With eyes glued to your picks of such good taste

They don't understand
What your movies mean to me
And how you suffer from your acne
Don't shut me out, I know you feel

What I feel, let's have a look at you
I won't judge you like they do

Now I have Betrayed you
Rented *Weekend at Bernie's II*
And though I didn't do it to spite you
On that movie rental night

You knew I'd picked a Gene's pick over yours
For I hurt your feelings, Vincent
You're strange and sensitive
And oh so beautiful, it's true

Movie rental night
Something special we had, thought you
You said you needed a few
Things from the store, so I'll bring them to you

Fireworks and cigarettes
The PLAY button off your VCR
Around my neck, give it back to Mom
But keep the vodka, I'll need it later on

They don't understand
What your movies mean to me
And how you suffer from your acne
I didn't know you were fifteen

I should have listened, turned around
When you said, "Go away – NOW!"

Told from the Elaine Benes character's point of view, these alternate lyrics are based on the *Seinfeld*, Season 8 episode "The Comeback." In this episode, Elaine falls in love with a mysterious employee at the video store, Vincent, who turns out to be a pimply teenager.

Haunted Haystack

A parody of the song "Something" *by the Beatles*

Some...Thing in the hay
It moves
Inside a stack that's like no other

Something evil lies
Within strawy roots
We don't want to fear it now
But light's seeping from the ground

No needle to be found

Some Thing in the hay
It knows
Through eyes unseen our every move

Some stench it emits
Makes us woozy
Putrid haze engulfs the farm
The horses bumble from the barn

No needle to be found

You're asking me why our hay glows
Why it grows, I don't know
Been mowed and dried yet roots drill low
Ceaseless growth
Uncontrolled

Some Thing splinters red
Barn wood
Eyes spiral dazed around we stumble

Some Thing's made our barn
A cavernous tomb
We can't help but fear it now
They're rising up from the ground

No needle to be found
Hay shadows spread 'cross town

A number-one hit in five countries—Australia, Canada, New Zealand, United States, and West Germany—"Something" marked the first time that a George Harrison composition became a Beatles A-side single.

Fairfield's Burning

The song "Scotland's Burning" (known in England as "London's Burning") is a variant of a popular children's nursery rhyme. It is said that the Scotland lyrics refer to the Burning of Edinburgh in 1544, as ordered by King Henry VIII of England. And it went like this:

Scotland's Burning

Scotland's burning
  Scotland's burning

Look out!
  Look out!

Fire, fire!
  Fire, fire!

Pour on water
  Pour on water

Fast forward to 1977, Massapequa, New York, Fairfield Elementary School, 4th grade General Music class. We would sing "Scotland's Burning" in a round, as it was intended to be sung. But outside of music class we sang this satirical parody (directed at our school, of course), which echoed through the hallways:

Fairfield's Burning

Fairfield's burning
  Fairfield's burning

Hooray!
  Hooray!

Fire, fire!
  Fire, fire!

Don't pour water
  Don't pour water

FeeT ACHe

A parody of the song "Heat Wave" *by Martha and the Vandellas*

Whenever I wear them
Feet squeezed inside
Start to hurting
As they fill with red fire
Could it be my shoes don't fit me
Or is this the pain I'm supposed to feel?

They make my feet ache
Hurting in my toes
I can't keep from crying
It's causing so much woe

Whenever I call his name,
"Dr. Scholl, ease the pain!"
Right now, right or left,
My feet feel lame, so inflamed
Will massaging gel insoles do the trick for me
Or should I see a doctor in podiatry?

Oh, how my feet ache
Doc, don't be callous
My broken metatarsals
Are tearing my feet apart

Sometimes I kneel and pray
Dismay all over my face
Can you explain it, alleviate it?
I ain't never felt such pain before
Now my pinky toe can't cry *wee wee wee*
All the way home, give me some better feet!

Balls of my feet ache
Morton's neuroma
I keep pulling and prying
But my shoes won't come off

Ow, ow, ow, ouch
Ow owwww, my corns!
Feet ache

Can't run, can't walk, can't dance.
Bunions, blisters, calluses
Making my feet ache
Feet ache, owwwwww!
Feet ache...

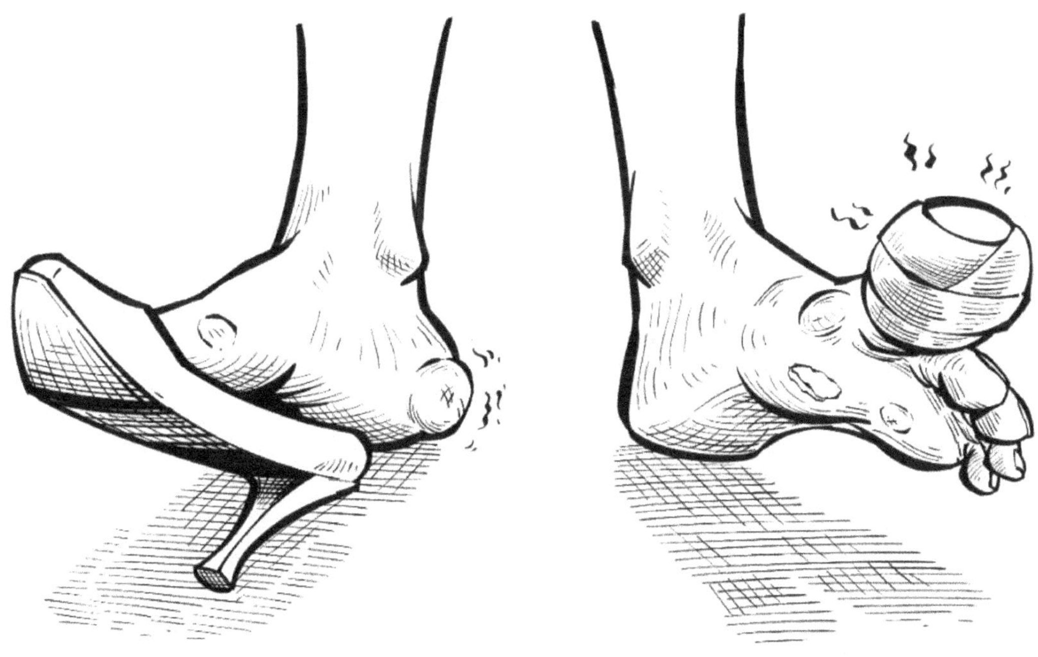

Its combination of gospel, jazz, and doo-wop made "Heat Wave" (aptly released in July 1963) one of the first songs to exemplify the music style later known as the "Motown Sound." The song earned a Grammy Award nomination, making Martha and the Vandellas the first Motown group ever to receive such an honor.

Washed Ashore

A parody of the song "Heart of Gold" *by Neil Young*

I've never been
On continents
I float for miles, never wash ashore
Every direction
Already been

I keep on hoping I'll be washed ashore
Never been before
Caught in currents, riptides uncontrolled
This is getting old

I've been through typhoons,
Tropical cyclones
Crossed over oceans but don't wash ashore
I cannot even find
Gilligan's Island

I keep on praying I'll be washed ashore
Waterlogged to the core
Caught in waves, I'm getting rocked and rolled
This is getting old

I keep on floating, never wash ashore
Just keep on floating, a shark ate my oar
My bottled message must have blown off course
I see the sky above and nothing more...

1972's "Heart of Gold," from the number-one album, *Harvest,* is the only U.S. number-one single by Canadian singer-songwriter Neil Young. It features backup vocals by James Taylor and Linda Ronstadt.

Hollandaise

A parody of the song "Holiday" *by Madonna*

Hollandaise, not mayonnaise
Hollandaise tastes so great.

If we took some hollandaise
Poured it on a quiche Lorraine
Oh yeah, that sounds first-rate
Or on eggs Benedict
Hol-lan-daise!
It would sate, sate our appetites.

Smothering steamed artichokes
It's gonna be a taste sensation
Perfect on cod smoked
Put some in my bouillabaisse

Let's all dine on
Delicately poached salmon, oh yeah
Blended butter, yolks, and lemon
Some salt and pepper
We need more hollandaise!

Hollandaise, not Béarnaise
Hollandaise, on my plate
We
have
got
to
make
some
more
Hollandaise, s'il vous plaît!

In the fall of 1983, Madonna served up her first mainstream hit single, "Holiday." It became an instant dancefloor smash, landing at number one on the *Billboard* Dance Club Songs chart.

We Never Tire of *Seinfeld*

A Seinfeld *parody of the song* "We Didn't Start the Fire" *by Billy Joel*

(Verse 1)
Larry David, "The Café"
Red dot, Art Vandelay
Smelly car, *Rochelle, Rochelle*
The Manssiere, The Bro

Kenny Rogers Roasters chicken
Soda, 7, "Something's missing."
Uncle Leo, gonorrhea
Toby's pinky toe

"Alec Berrrg," Mandelbaum
Bubble Boy, Van Nostrand
T-Bone, "The Pool Guy"
Tossing up a marble rye

"Holy cow!", "Rusty!"
Kramerica Industries
Beefarino, "Hoochie mama!"
"Yo-yo ma!", The Rabbi

(Chorus 1)
George didn't start "The Fire."
It was burgers burning
Sent the guests all hurling
George didn't start "The Fire."
Though he might have guided,
Shoved them all aside

(Verse 2)
Chocolate babka, Jon Voight's car
Frogger, pits of Mackinaws
Braless Wonder, pig-man, "Stell*aaa!*"
Pony remark

Lloyd Braun, Eric the Clown
Tuscany, "Downtown"
Japanese in drawers
"All they do is mock!"

"The Pie", "The Keys"
"You're the wind beneath my wings."
Candy line-up, butter tan
"The Library", the Assman

"Helloooo", "The Contest"
Superman allusions
Parking space, *Melrose Place*
Chunnel at two theaters

(Chorus 2)
George loves Marisa Tomei
Was caught fantasizing
In a pillow pile
George loves Marisa Tomei
And though Susan died,
George has no complaints

(Verse 3)
Little Rock, "The Heart Attack"
Mickey Abbott, Todd Gack
"The Pick", Jerry's wife
Kramer's hansom cab rides

"Giddy-up!", Jean-Paul Jean-Paul
Farfel, Danny Tartabull
"Heartbreaker", rickshaw ride
Jackie Chiles, *TV Guide*

Svenjolly, "The Slicer"
JFK's golf clubs
Nazi soups, Bosco
The Wiz, "Desperado"

Koko the Monkey
"The Limo", David Puddy
Mr. Kruger, Maestro
Bubblegum in bagel dough

(Chorus 3)
George tries but can't get fired
From the New York Yankees
Dripping with strawberries
George tries but can't get fired

Drags the trophy around
While he howls and scowls

(Verse 4)
Dr. Whatley, Feldman
Mr. Pitt, "Can't-stand-ya!"
Lippman, Peterman
Susan Ross Foundation

GI Joe, L-tryptophan
Ring in the Newmanium
"The Bris", "The Pen"
Jerry beats Duncan

"No soup for you, *next!*"
Put the gang under arrest
Steinbrenner blowwwn away!
Eggplant calzone every day

(Chorus 4)
George likes his fridge recliner
He was decompressing
After doing nothing
George likes his fridge recliner
Though "The Summer of George"
Never quite transpired

(Verse 5)
Moviefone, Poppie, Ping
Kenny Bania back again
Nip shot, hot tub
Bob Cobb, Friar's Club

Box of raisins, "Manya died!"
Kramer painting road lines
Babu Bhatt from Pakistan
Chinese gum, Bodysuit Man

"Goodbye, Norman!", "Worlds collide!"
Newman attempts suicide
Keith Hernandez, airport bets
AIDS Walk, Festivus

Aaron, Dan, the low talker
The Good Samaritan law

Crazy Joe Davola's walls
Elaine in the bathroom stall

("The Finale")
We never tire of *Seinfeld*
For a show about nothing
It was really something!
We laugh so hard at *Seinfeld*
"Yada, yada, yada"
Syndication will go on and on and on and on and on...

This parody represents 129 of the 180 episodes of the sitcom *Seinfeld* from all nine seasons, inclusive, which aired from 1989 to 1998. Among its many references are 59 characters, 19 foods, 17 quotes from the show, 15 formal episode titles (and parts of others), eight media titles, and a few of George Costanza's and Cosmo Kramer's alter egos.

ABOUT THE AUTHOR

Ronald A. Busse is a professional writer and poet. His children's picture book *Where Is the Beach?* was published in 2024 by Newman Springs Publishing. He has also written *Poems That Could End the World* (Turning Point, 2020), a poetry collection nominated for an Elgin Award by the Science Fiction & Fantasy Poetry Association.

All three of Busse's books are available at www.Amazon.com. To order autographed copies of *The Parody Project, Where Is the Beach?* and *Poems That Could End the World*, please contact him @ronbuswriter@aol.com.

Nearly one hundred of Busse's poems have appeared individually in various publications in Australia, Canada, Scotland, England, India, and the United States. He is an accomplished freelance writer and editor who also markets other writers' work to publishers. His first poetry book, *Into the Retrospectrum* (now out of print), was released in 1997.

Equally passionate about music, Busse enjoys playing a variety of musical instruments including the trumpet, keyboards, harmonica, and melodica. He resides in Denver, Colorado with his two feline companions, Little Johnny Jet and Gary.

Keep on Smiling!

ALSO AVAILABLE FROM

RONALD A. BUSSE

Where Is the Beach? is a delightful picture book adventure, whose story invites young readers to follow along on the escapades of Puppy, who sets out to find the beach in a hot-air balloon! Through Puppy's journey, children will find inspiration to embrace curiosity, seek guidance, and cherish the joy of discovery. *Full description at Amazon.com.*

Delve into the darkness of ***Poems That Could End the World***, a gripping collection of speculative poetry, embracing science-fiction and horror! Encounter eeriness in alien life, death, environment and climate change, through numerous traditional poetry forms, each defined in a handy Poetic Form Index!
Full description at Amazon.com.

Available at Amazon.com!
To order* autographed copies, *please contact Ronald at ronbuswriter@aol.com!

www.ingramcontent.com/pod-product-compliance
Lightning Source LLC
Chambersburg PA
CBHW041051050726
47599CB00018B/2104
* 9 7 8 1 9 6 9 8 1 8 2 6 4 *